NYCTOPHOBIA: OUT OF THE DARKNESS

A Practical Approach to Overcoming Your Fear of the Dark

Asa Eccleston Kibilski

CONTENTS

WHAT IS NYCTOPHOBIA?

It's the middle of the night. You're lying in bed, the room pitch black except for the sliver of moonlight filtering through the curtains. Every creak of the house, every rustle of leaves outside the window, sends a jolt of fear through you. Your heart pounds, your breath quickens, and your mind races with terrifying images. Sound familiar? If so, you're not alone.

You might be experiencing nyctophobia, or the fear of the dark.

It's more common than you think. Many people, both children and adults, experience some level of discomfort or anxiety in the dark. But for those with nyctophobia, this fear can be overwhelming, impacting daily life and leading to significant distress.

So, what exactly is nyctophobia?

Nyctophobia is classified as an anxiety disorder. It's characterized by an intense, irrational fear of the dark or nighttime. This fear is often disproportionate to the actual danger and can trigger a range of physical and emotional symptoms, including:

- **Physical:** Rapid heartbeat, sweating, trembling, shortness of breath, nausea, dizziness
- **Emotional:** Feelings of panic, dread, helplessness, and a loss of control

It's important to remember that experiencing some fear of the dark is completely normal, especially in childhood. Evolutionarily, it makes sense! Darkness used to hide real threats, and our brains are wired to be cautious.

However, when this fear becomes excessive, persistent, and starts interfering with your daily life, it's time to take it seriously.

How do you know if your fear is "normal" or something more?

Think about how your fear of the dark affects you. Does it:

- Prevent you from sleeping alone?
- Make you avoid going out at night?
- Cause significant distress during power outages?
- Lead to you constantly checking for "monsters" or imagined threats?
- Interfere with your social activities or relationships?

If you answered yes to any of these questions, it's possible that you're dealing with nyctophobia.

But there's good news!

Nyctophobia is a treatable condition. This book will provide you with the knowledge, tools, and strategies you need to overcome your fear of the dark and reclaim your life.

In the following chapters, we'll explore the causes of nyctophobia, delve into practical techniques for managing anxiety, and guide you on a journey from fear to freedom.

You don't have to live in the shadows of fear any longer. Take a deep breath, and let's embark on this journey together.

WHY AM I AFRAID OF THE DARK?

In the last chapter, we explored what nyctophobia is and how it might be affecting you. Now, let's dive deeper into the "why" behind this fear. Understanding the roots of your nyctophobia is a crucial step towards overcoming it.

Think of it like this: you can't effectively fight an enemy you don't understand, right? The same goes for fear. By understanding where it comes from, we can start to dismantle it.

So, what causes nyctophobia?

Well, it's rarely just one thing. It's usually a combination of factors that intertwine to create this fear. Let's explore some of the most common culprits:

1. Early Childhood Experiences:

Think back to your childhood. Were there any specific incidents that might have triggered your fear of the dark? Perhaps:

- You were often left alone in the dark as a child.
- You experienced a traumatic event at night, like a burglary or a bad dream.
- You were told scary stories or shown frightening images related to the dark.

Our early experiences, especially those involving fear and anxiety, can leave a lasting impact on our brains. These experiences can shape our perceptions and create associations between darkness and danger, even if those associations are not based on reality.

2. Learned Behavior:

Sometimes, we learn to be afraid of the dark by observing others. If your parents or caregivers were anxious about the dark, you might have unconsciously adopted their fear.

Think about it: children are incredibly perceptive. They pick up on subtle cues from the adults around them. If a parent constantly checks under the bed or expresses fear about being alone at night, a child may internalize these behaviors and develop a similar fear.

3. Evolutionary Factors:

As we mentioned in the previous chapter, fear of the dark is, to some extent, ingrained in our DNA. For our ancestors, darkness was a genuine source of danger. Predators lurked in the shadows, and navigating unfamiliar terrain at night was risky.

This primal fear may still linger within us, even though we no longer face the same threats. Our modern brains, however, sometimes struggle to distinguish between real and imagined dangers, leading to anxiety in situations that are objectively safe.

4. Overactive Imagination:

When we can't see clearly, our imagination tends to fill in the gaps. This can be a wonderful thing when we're daydreaming or engaging in creative pursuits. But for someone with nyctophobia, an overactive imagination can conjure up terrifying images and scenarios in the dark.

Our minds can be incredibly powerful, and sometimes they work against us. If you're prone to anxiety, your mind might create a constant stream of "what if" scenarios, fueling your fear of the dark.

5. Underlying Anxiety or Other Mental Health Conditions:

Nyctophobia can sometimes be a symptom of a broader anxiety disorder or other mental health conditions. For example, people with generalized anxiety disorder (GAD), post-traumatic stress disorder (PTSD), or obsessive-compulsive disorder (OCD) may be more prone to developing nyctophobia.

If you suspect that your fear of the dark might be linked to an underlying mental health condition, it's essential to seek professional help. A therapist can help you identify the root cause of your anxiety and develop a personalized treatment plan.

Understanding Your Unique Story

While these are some of the common causes of nyctophobia, it's important to remember that everyone's experience is unique. Your fear of the dark may stem from a combination of these factors, or it may have a completely different origin.

Take some time to reflect on your own experiences and try to identify any patterns or triggers that contribute to your fear. This self-reflection will be invaluable as you move forward on your journey to overcome nyctophobia.

In the next chapter, we'll explore how nyctophobia affects different aspects of your life and why it's so important to address this fear.

THE IMPACT OF FEAR

We've talked about what nyctophobia is and where it might come from. Now, let's get real about how this fear can actually affect your life.

You might be thinking, "It's just a fear of the dark, right?" But the truth is, nyctophobia can cast a long shadow, impacting many different areas of your life in ways you might not even realize.

1. Sleep Disturbances:

This one might seem obvious, but it's worth emphasizing. Nyctophobia can make it incredibly difficult to fall asleep and stay asleep. The anticipation of darkness can trigger anxiety, leading to a vicious cycle of worry and sleeplessness.

Imagine this: you're exhausted after a long day, but as soon as you turn off the lights, your mind starts racing. You toss and turn, your heart pounding, unable to relax. This can lead to chronic sleep deprivation, which in turn can affect your mood, concentration, and overall well-being.

2. Social Limitations:

Nyctophobia can make it challenging to participate in social activities that take place at night. Dinner with friends, going to the movies, or even just taking an evening stroll might feel impossible if the thought of being in the dark fills you with dread.

This can lead to feelings of isolation and loneliness, as you may start to withdraw from social situations to avoid your fear. You might decline invitations, make excuses, or even cancel plans at the last minute, which can strain your relationships and leave you feeling disconnected.

3. Travel Restrictions:

Imagine wanting to explore a new city or go camping under the stars, but your fear of the dark holds you back. Nyctophobia can significantly limit your travel experiences, preventing you from enjoying activities and destinations that involve nighttime settings.

Even something as simple as staying in a hotel room can become a source of anxiety if you're afraid of the dark. Unfamiliar surroundings, combined with the darkness, can heighten your fear and make it difficult to relax and enjoy your trip.

4. Impact on Daily Activities:

Nyctophobia doesn't just affect you at night. It can seep into your daily life in subtle ways. You might avoid going to the basement, taking out the trash after dark, or even walking to your car in a dimly lit parking lot.

These seemingly small things can add up and create a sense of restriction and limitation in your life. You might feel like you're constantly on edge, always aware of the level of light around you, and always anticipating the next moment when darkness will descend.

5. Emotional Well-being:

Living with a constant fear can take a toll on your emotional health. Nyctophobia can lead to feelings of anxiety, helplessness, and even shame. You might feel like you're "different" or "childish" for being afraid of the dark, which can impact your self-esteem.

It's important to remember that you're not alone and that your feelings are valid. Seeking help for nyctophobia is a sign of strength, not weakness. By addressing this fear, you're taking a positive step towards improving your overall well-being and living a fuller, more fulfilling life.

Breaking Free from the Shadows

Nyctophobia can cast a long shadow, but it doesn't have to define you. By understanding the impact this fear has on your life, you can start to take back control.

In the next chapter, we'll dive into the specific triggers that can set off your fear of the dark, helping you to gain a deeper understanding of your individual experience with nyctophobia.

TRIGGERS

We've explored the "what" and the "why" of nyctophobia, and we've seen how this fear can impact your daily life. Now, let's get a little more specific. In this chapter, we'll shine a light on those pesky triggers—the things that set off your fear of the dark.

Think of triggers as the sparks that ignite the fire of your fear. They can be external (things in your environment) or internal (thoughts and feelings). By identifying your unique triggers, you can start to anticipate and manage them more effectively.

External Triggers:

These are the things in your surroundings that can activate your fear response. For many people with nyctophobia, complete darkness is a major trigger. The absence of any light can create a sense of disorientation and vulnerability, making it easier for fear to take hold.

Shadows can also be quite triggering. They can be deceiving, playing tricks on our eyes and making us see things that aren't really there. Our imaginations can run wild, transforming ordinary shadows into menacing shapes.

Think about how you feel in unfamiliar environments at night. Being in a new place can heighten anxiety, especially in the dark. You might feel less secure and more vulnerable when you're not familiar with your surroundings.

Certain sounds can also be amplified in the dark and trigger a fear response. Creaking floorboards, rustling leaves, the howling wind—our brains are wired to pay attention to unusual sounds at night, as they could signal danger.

Finally, consider the role of isolation. Being alone in the dark can be particularly frightening for some people. The feeling of isolation can amplify existing fears and make you feel more vulnerable.

Internal Triggers:

These are the thoughts, feelings, and sensations that can contribute to your fear of the dark. One of the most common internal triggers is imagined threats. Our minds can be our own worst enemies, conjuring up terrifying images and scenarios in the dark. You might worry about intruders, monsters, or other imagined dangers lurking in the shadows.

Negative thoughts can also fuel your fear and make it harder to cope. "What if something bad happens?" "I can't handle this." "I'm going to lose control." These types of thoughts can spiral, increasing your anxiety.

Pay attention to your physical sensations. Sometimes, physical sensations like a racing heart, shortness of breath, or dizziness can trigger a fear response. Your body might be interpreting these sensations as signs of danger, even if there's no real threat present.

Past experiences can also play a role. Memories of past traumatic events or frightening experiences in the dark can resurface and trigger anxiety.

Finally, consider how your overall stress and anxiety levels affect your fear of the dark. When you're already feeling stressed or anxious, your fear might be more intense. Stress can lower your tolerance for uncertainty and make you more susceptible to fear.

Identifying Your Triggers:

Now that you have a better understanding of potential triggers, it's time to do some detective work and identify your own personal triggers. Keep a "fear journal" and record your experiences with nyctophobia. Each time you feel anxious in the dark, write down what happened, where you were, what you were thinking, and how you felt physically. Reflect on your past and any experiences that might have contributed to your fear of the dark. Were there any specific events or situations that stand out? Pay attention to your body and notice how it reacts in different situations. Do certain sounds or sensations trigger a fear response?

By becoming more aware of your triggers, you can start to develop strategies for managing them. In the next chapter, we'll explore some practical techniques for overcoming your fear of the dark and taking back control.

KNOW YOUR FEARS

We've come a long way together! We've explored what nyctophobia is, delved into its potential causes, and even uncovered those sneaky triggers that can set off your fear. Now, it's time to turn the spotlight inward and really get to know your fears.

This chapter is all about self-discovery and understanding. Think of it as your own personal "fear investigation." By taking the time to explore your fears in a structured way, you'll gain valuable insights that will help you on your journey to overcoming nyctophobia.

Why is self-assessment important?

Think of it like this: you wouldn't set off on a road trip without a map, would you? Similarly, you need a map of your fears to navigate your way out of the darkness. Self-assessment provides that map. It helps you:

- **Pinpoint your specific fears:** What exactly are you afraid of? Is it the darkness itself, or is it the perceived dangers that lurk within it? Are you afraid of being alone, or are you afraid of something specific happening?
- **Identify patterns and connections:** Are there any common themes or patterns in your fear responses? Do certain situations or thoughts consistently trigger your anxiety?
- **Track your progress:** As you work through this book and implement the strategies we'll discuss, self-assessment will help you monitor your progress and celebrate your successes.
- **Empower yourself:** By understanding your fears, you take away some of their power. Knowledge is power, and the more

you know about your fears, the better equipped you'll be to face them.

How to conduct your "fear investigation":

There are a few different tools you can use to explore your fears. Here are two of the most effective:

1. Journaling:

Grab a notebook and pen, or open a document on your computer, and start writing. There are no rules here, just let your thoughts and feelings flow. Here are some prompts to get you started:

- Describe your earliest memories of being afraid of the dark.
- What specific thoughts or images come to mind when you're in the dark?
- How does your body feel when you experience fear?
- What situations or environments trigger your fear the most?
- What do you think would happen if you faced your fear?

Don't worry about grammar or spelling, just focus on expressing yourself honestly. The act of writing itself can be therapeutic, helping you to process your emotions and gain clarity.

2. Self-Assessment Questions:

Here are some questions to ponder and answer in your journal or simply reflect on:

- On a scale of 1 to 10, how intense is your fear of the dark in different situations (e.g., at home, in a new place, alone, with others)?
- What coping mechanisms do you currently use to manage your fear (e.g., leaving a light on, sleeping with a companion, avoiding the dark)?
- What are your goals for overcoming your fear? What would you like to be able to do that you can't do now because of your fear?

Embrace the Process

This self-assessment process might feel a little uncomfortable at times, but that's okay. It's normal to feel some resistance when confronting your fears. Remember to be patient with yourself and approach this exploration with curiosity and compassion.

The insights you gain from this self-assessment will be invaluable as you move forward. You'll have a clearer understanding of your fears, your triggers, and your goals, which will help you to choose the most effective strategies for overcoming nyctophobia.

In the next chapter, we'll start exploring those strategies, beginning with powerful cognitive techniques for managing your fear.

CHALLENGE YOUR THOUGHTS

Up until now, we've focused on understanding your fear – where it comes from, how it affects you, and what triggers it. Now, it's time to start taking action! This chapter introduces you to the incredible power of your mind and how you can use it to challenge those fear-based thoughts that keep you trapped in the shadows.

You see, fear isn't just an emotion; it's a thought process. When you're afraid of the dark, your mind is likely flooded with negative thoughts and "what if" scenarios. "What if there's someone hiding in the closet?" "What if I can't see and I trip and fall?" "What if I have a panic attack and no one can help me?"

These thoughts, while understandable, are often exaggerated and unrealistic. They're like those distorted mirrors at a carnival – they make things seem much scarier than they actually are.

Cognitive techniques are like a toolkit for your mind. They help you identify these distorted thoughts, challenge their validity, and replace them with more realistic and positive ones.

1. Identify Your Negative Thoughts:

The first step is to become aware of your negative thought patterns. Remember that fear journal we talked about? It's a great tool for this. When you feel anxious in the dark, take a moment to write down the thoughts that are running through your head.

You might notice themes emerging. Maybe you tend to catastrophize, imagining the worst possible outcome. Or perhaps you engage in "black and white" thinking, believing that if you're not completely safe, you're in imminent danger.

2. Challenge the Validity of Your Thoughts:

Once you've identified your negative thoughts, it's time to put them on trial. Ask yourself:

- Is this thought really true? What evidence do I have to support it?
- Is there another way to look at this situation?
- What would I tell a friend who was having this thought?

For example, if you're thinking, "I can't handle being alone in the dark," challenge that thought. Have you ever been alone in the dark before? Did you survive? What coping mechanisms did you use? Remind yourself of your strength and resilience.

3. Replace Negative Thoughts with Positive Ones:

Now comes the fun part – replacing those fear-based thoughts with more positive and empowering ones. This takes practice, but it gets easier over time.

Instead of thinking, "I'm going to panic if the lights go out," try thinking, "I've handled this before, and I can handle it again. I have tools and techniques to manage my anxiety."

4. Practice, Practice, Practice:

Challenging your thoughts is like learning a new skill. It takes time and repetition. The more you practice, the better you'll become at recognizing and reframing those negative thoughts.

Here are some additional tips to help you along the way:

- **Be patient with yourself:** It takes time to change your thinking patterns. Don't get discouraged if you don't see results overnight.
- **Start small:** Begin by challenging one or two negative thoughts at a time.
- **Use affirmations:** Create positive statements about yourself and your ability to overcome your fear. Repeat them daily,

even when you don't fully believe them.
- **Seek support:** Talk to a therapist or trusted friend about your fears and your thought patterns. They can offer guidance and encouragement.

By mastering the art of challenging your thoughts, you'll be well on your way to conquering your fear of the dark. In the next chapter, we'll explore another powerful tool: gradual exposure therapy.

FACING THE DARKNESS

Okay, deep breath! We're about to step into the realm of action. In the last chapter, we learned how to challenge those fear-based thoughts. Now, we're going to gently, and at your own pace, start facing the darkness itself.

This is where **gradual exposure therapy** comes in. It's a proven technique for overcoming phobias, and it works by gradually exposing you to the thing you fear, in this case, the dark.

Think of it like climbing a mountain. You wouldn't try to summit Everest on your first day of hiking, right? You'd start with smaller hills, gradually building your strength and confidence. That's exactly what we'll do with your fear of the dark.

The key to gradual exposure therapy is to take it slow and steady. We're not going to throw you into a pitch-black room and lock the door. Instead, we'll create a step-by-step plan, starting with situations that cause minimal anxiety and gradually working our way up to more challenging ones.

Here's how to create your exposure ladder:

1. **Identify your fear hierarchy:** Make a list of situations related to darkness that trigger your anxiety, ranging from the least scary to the most scary.

   For example:

   - Sitting in a dimly lit room
   - Turning off the lights in your bedroom for a few seconds

- o   Walking down a hallway with the lights off
- o   Spending 5 minutes in a dark room
- o   Sleeping in complete darkness

2. **Start with the easiest step:** Begin with the situation that causes the least amount of anxiety. Stay in that situation until your anxiety starts to decrease. This might take a few minutes, or it might take longer. The important thing is to stay with it until you feel some relief.

3. **Gradually move up the ladder:** Once you feel comfortable with the first step, move on to the next one. Continue this process, gradually exposing yourself to more challenging situations as your confidence grows.

4. **Celebrate your successes:** Each time you complete a step on your exposure ladder, take a moment to acknowledge your courage and celebrate your progress. You're doing amazing!

Tips for successful exposure:

- **Use relaxation techniques:** Before and during exposure, practice relaxation techniques like deep breathing or progressive muscle relaxation to help manage your anxiety.
- **Bring a friend:** If you feel more comfortable, ask a trusted friend or family member to support you during your exposure exercises.
- **Distract yourself:** If your anxiety becomes overwhelming, try distracting yourself with a book, music, or a calming activity.
- **Don't give up:** There might be times when you feel like giving up. That's okay. Just take a break and try again later. Remember, progress is not always linear.

Exposure therapy is a powerful tool for overcoming fear, but it's important to remember that it's not a quick fix. It takes time, patience, and commitment. But with each step you take, you'll be moving closer to a life free from the grip of nyctophobia.

In the next chapter, we'll explore another set of tools for managing anxiety: relaxation and mindfulness exercises.

RELAX AND BREATHE

We've been talking about facing your fears and challenging your thoughts, which are incredibly important steps in overcoming nyctophobia. But now, let's shift gears a bit and focus on calming your body and mind.

Imagine this: you're about to turn off the lights, and your heart starts pounding, your palms get sweaty, and your mind races with anxious thoughts. Sound familiar? This is your body's fight-or-flight response kicking in. It's a natural reaction to perceived danger, but when it comes to nyctophobia, this response is often triggered unnecessarily.

That's where relaxation and mindfulness exercises come in. These techniques help you to soothe your nervous system, reduce anxiety, and gain control over your fear response.

1. Deep Breathing:

This might seem simple, but deep breathing is one of the most effective ways to calm your body and mind. When you're anxious, your breathing tends to become shallow and rapid. Deep breathing helps to slow your heart rate, lower your blood pressure, and relax your muscles.

Here's a simple exercise to try:

- Find a comfortable position, either sitting or lying down.
- Close your eyes and place one hand on your chest and the other on your stomach.
- Inhale slowly and deeply through your nose, feeling your stomach rise as you fill your lungs with air.
- Exhale slowly through your mouth, feeling your stomach fall as you release the air.

- Repeat this for several minutes, focusing on the sensation of your breath entering and leaving your body.

2. Progressive Muscle Relaxation:

This technique involves systematically tensing and relaxing different muscle groups in your body. It helps to release physical tension and promote a sense of calm.

Here's how it works:

- Start by tensing the muscles in your toes for a few seconds, then release.
- Move up to your calves, tensing and relaxing them.
- Continue this process, working your way up your body, tensing and relaxing each muscle group (legs, abdomen, chest, arms, shoulders, neck, and face).

3. Mindfulness Meditation:

Mindfulness is all about paying attention to the present moment without judgment. It helps you to become more aware of your thoughts, feelings, and sensations without getting carried away by them.

There are many different ways to practice mindfulness. You can try a guided meditation app, listen to calming music, or simply focus on your breath or your senses. The key is to bring your attention back to the present moment whenever your mind starts to wander.

4. Visualization:

Visualization involves creating a mental picture of a calming and peaceful scene. This can help to reduce anxiety and promote relaxation.

Close your eyes and imagine yourself in a place where you feel safe and secure. It could be a beach, a forest, or your own cozy bedroom. Engage all your senses – what do you see, hear, smell, taste, and feel?

Making it a Habit:

The key to reaping the benefits of these relaxation techniques is to practice them regularly, even when you're not feeling anxious. Make them a part of your daily routine, just like brushing your teeth or taking a shower.

You can also use these techniques in the moment, whenever you feel your anxiety rising. If you're about to turn off the lights and you feel a surge of fear, take a few deep breaths, practice progressive muscle relaxation, or visualize a calming scene.

By incorporating relaxation and mindfulness into your life, you'll be building a powerful arsenal of tools to manage your anxiety and face your fear of the dark with greater ease.

In the next chapter, we'll explore another powerful technique: visualization.

VISUALIZE AND CONQUER

Close your eyes for a moment. Imagine yourself in a peaceful meadow bathed in warm sunlight. A gentle breeze rustles through the leaves, and birds sing sweetly in the distance. Can you feel the soft grass beneath your feet and the sun warming your skin?

This, my friend, is the power of visualization. It's the ability to create vivid mental images that can transport you to another place, evoke positive emotions, and even help you overcome your fears.

In this chapter, we'll explore how you can use visualization to conquer your fear of the dark and create a sense of peace and safety, even in the absence of light.

Why Visualization Works

Our brains are incredibly powerful. They can't always distinguish between real experiences and imagined ones. When you visualize a calming scene, your brain responds as if you were actually there, releasing feel-good chemicals like endorphins and serotonin.

This can help to reduce anxiety, lower your heart rate, and promote relaxation. But visualization can do more than just calm you down. It can also help you to:

- **Challenge negative thoughts:** If you tend to imagine scary scenarios in the dark, visualization can help you to replace those images with more positive ones.
- **Build confidence:** By visualizing yourself successfully facing your fears, you can increase your self-belief and your ability to cope.

- **Create a sense of control:** When you feel like your fear is controlling you, visualization can help you to regain a sense of agency and empowerment.

Creating Your Visualization Sanctuary

Now, let's create your own visualization sanctuary. This is a safe and peaceful place that you can access anytime you feel anxious or afraid.

1. **Choose your setting:** Think about a place where you feel completely at ease. It could be a real place you've visited, or it could be a place you create in your imagination. Some popular choices include a beach, a forest, a mountaintop, or a cozy room.

2. **Engage your senses:** As you visualize your sanctuary, bring it to life with sensory details. What do you see, hear, smell, taste, and feel? The more vivid your visualization, the more effective it will be.

3. **Add a touch of magic:** This is your sanctuary, so feel free to get creative! Maybe there's a waterfall cascading down a cliff, or a friendly animal curled up beside you. Let your imagination soar.

4. **Practice regularly:** The more you practice visualizing your sanctuary, the easier it will be to access it when you need it. Make it a part of your daily routine, or use it whenever you feel anxious.

Visualizing Success

In addition to creating a general sanctuary, you can also use visualization to practice facing your fears.

- **Imagine yourself in a dark room:** Start by visualizing yourself in a situation that triggers mild anxiety, like sitting in a dimly lit room. See yourself feeling calm and relaxed, even in the absence of bright light.

- **Gradually increase the challenge:** As you become more comfortable, gradually increase the challenge in your visualizations. Imagine yourself walking down a dark hallway, turning off the lights in your bedroom, or even sleeping in complete darkness.
- **Focus on positive outcomes:** Visualize yourself successfully navigating these situations, feeling confident and in control. See yourself overcoming your fear and enjoying the peace and tranquility of the darkness.

Visualization is a powerful tool that can help you to transform your relationship with the dark. By creating a mental sanctuary and visualizing yourself overcoming your fears, you can build resilience, reduce anxiety, and reclaim your peace of mind.

CREATE A SLEEP SANCTUARY

We've been exploring a lot of powerful tools for managing your fear of the dark, from challenging your thoughts to facing your fears head-on. But let's not forget about one of the most important aspects of overcoming nyctophobia: creating a sleep sanctuary.

After all, your bedroom is where you likely spend the most time in the dark. It's where you rest, recharge, and prepare for the day ahead. If your bedroom feels like a battleground against the darkness, it's going to be much harder to overcome your fear.

So, let's transform your bedroom into a haven of peace and tranquility, a place where you feel safe, secure, and ready to embrace the night.

Set the Mood with Light:

While we're working towards embracing the darkness, a little bit of calming light can go a long way in creating a soothing atmosphere. Install a dimmer switch on your main light fixture so you can control the brightness and gradually adjust the light level as you prepare for sleep. A small nightlight can also provide just enough illumination to ease your anxiety without disrupting your sleep. Choose a warm, soft light rather than a harsh, blue light. And if you're feeling creative, consider adding some fairy lights or string lights. These can add a touch of whimsy and create a relaxing ambiance. Drape them around your headboard, windows, or even across the ceiling.

Embrace Comfort and Calm:

Your bedroom should be a haven of comfort and relaxation. Invest in soft, cozy bedding that makes you feel pampered and secure. Choose calming colors and textures that promote relaxation. Make sure your bedroom is cool and well-ventilated, as a slightly cooler temperature can promote better sleep. Aromatherapy can also be a powerful tool for relaxation. Use a diffuser with calming essential oils like lavender, chamomile, or sandalwood. Finally, remember that clutter can be a source of stress and anxiety. Keep your bedroom tidy and organized to create a sense of calm and order.

Minimize Distractions:

Your bedroom should be a sanctuary for sleep, not a hub for activity. Keep electronic devices out of the bedroom, or at least turn them off an hour before bedtime. The blue light emitted from screens can interfere with your sleep. Avoid working or studying in your bedroom, as this can create an association between your bedroom and stress. If outside noise is an issue, use earplugs or a white noise machine to block out any distracting sounds.

Create a Bedtime Ritual:

A consistent bedtime ritual can signal to your body and mind that it's time to wind down and prepare for sleep. Take a warm bath to relax your muscles, read a calming book to quiet your mind, or listen to relaxing music to soothe your senses. You can also incorporate deep breathing, progressive muscle relaxation, or mindfulness meditation into your bedtime routine.

Personalize Your Space:

Make your bedroom a reflection of your personality and your needs. Surround yourself with things that bring you joy and comfort. This might include photos of loved ones, inspiring artwork, plants, or even crystals.

By creating a sleep sanctuary that feels safe, comfortable, and inviting, you'll be taking a major step towards overcoming your fear of the dark. Your bedroom will become a place where you can truly relax, recharge, and embrace the night.

BEYOND THE BEDROOM

Congratulations! You've been working hard, creating a sleep sanctuary, challenging your thoughts, and even facing the darkness head-on. But nyctophobia doesn't just stay confined to your bedroom, does it? It can creep into other areas of your life, holding you back from experiences and adventures.

This chapter is all about expanding your comfort zone and taking your newfound confidence beyond those bedroom walls. We'll explore how to navigate different environments and situations that might trigger your fear, so you can truly start living a life free from the limitations of nyctophobia.

Conquering the Outdoors:

Think about those times when the fear might strike outside your home. Maybe it's walking to your car in a dimly lit parking lot, taking an evening stroll through the park, or even just stepping out onto your porch at night. Start by venturing out in areas you know well, like your own backyard or a well-lit street in your neighborhood. Gradually, as you feel more comfortable, you can begin to explore new environments.

Bringing a friend or family member along can provide a sense of security and support. Focus on your senses to ground yourself in the present moment. Listen to the sounds of nature, feel the cool breeze on your skin, and notice the smells around you. A flashlight can be a helpful tool to illuminate your path and reduce anxiety. And if you feel your anxiety rising, remember those mindfulness techniques we discussed - take a few deep breaths and focus on the present moment.

Navigating Social Situations:

Nyctophobia can sometimes make it difficult to participate in social activities that take place at night. Dinner with friends, going to the movies, or attending a party might feel overwhelming if the thought of being in the dark triggers your fear.

Open communication with your friends is key. Let them know about your fear and how it affects you. True friends will be understanding and supportive. When making plans, suggest restaurants or other venues with ample lighting. Arriving early can also help you to get acclimated to the environment before it gets too dark. Once you're there, focus on the company and engage in conversations and activities that distract you from your fear and help you to enjoy the social interaction. And if you feel overwhelmed, don't hesitate to excuse yourself for a few minutes to step outside or find a quieter space.

Embracing New Experiences:

As you gain confidence, consider embracing new experiences that might have previously seemed out of reach. Maybe you've always wanted to go camping under the stars, attend an outdoor concert, or visit a nocturnal zoo.

Start small, perhaps with activities that involve minimal darkness, like an evening picnic or a sunset hike. Do your research and learn as much as you can about the activity or environment beforehand. This can help to reduce anxiety and increase your sense of control. It's also helpful to anticipate potential challenges and develop coping strategies. For example, if you're going camping, bring a headlamp and extra batteries. Most importantly, focus on the positive! Remember why you want to have this experience and focus on the positive aspects. And when you do venture out, celebrate your courage in stepping outside your comfort zone and trying something new.

Remember, overcoming nyctophobia is a journey, not a destination. There will be ups and downs along the way. But with each step you take, you'll be gaining more confidence and freedom. By venturing beyond the bedroom and facing your fears in different environments, you'll be proving to yourself that you can handle the darkness, no matter where you are.

SLEEP CYCLES

We've talked a lot about managing fear and anxiety, but let's not forget that nyctophobia often goes hand-in-hand with sleep disturbances. It's a bit of a chicken-and-egg situation, isn't it? Fear of the dark can disrupt your sleep, and lack of sleep can make your anxiety worse.

So, in this chapter, we're going to delve into the fascinating world of sleep cycles and explore how understanding your body's natural rhythms can help you conquer nyctophobia and achieve more restful nights.

The Rhythm of the Night: Understanding Your Sleep Cycles

Your sleep isn't just a single, continuous state. It's a dynamic process that cycles through different stages throughout the night. These stages, broadly categorized as REM (rapid eye movement) and non-REM sleep, each play a crucial role in your physical and mental well-being.

Non-REM sleep is divided into three stages:

1. **Light sleep:** This is the transitional stage between wakefulness and sleep, where you might experience muscle twitches and a slowing of your heart rate.

2. **Deep sleep:** This is the most restorative stage of sleep, crucial for physical repair and growth. It's harder to wake up from this stage, and you might feel groggy if you do.

3. **Deepest sleep:** This stage is similar to deep sleep, with even slower brain waves and a further reduction in heart

rate and breathing.

REM sleep is when your brain activity increases, and you experience vivid dreams. This stage is essential for learning, memory consolidation, and emotional processing.

Throughout the night, you cycle through these stages multiple times, with each cycle lasting about 90 minutes.

How Nyctophobia Disrupts Your Sleep Cycle

When you're afraid of the dark, your anxiety can make it difficult to fall asleep and stay asleep. You might find yourself tossing and turning, worrying about imagined threats, or experiencing physical symptoms like a racing heart or shortness of breath. This can prevent you from entering the deeper, more restorative stages of sleep, leaving you feeling tired and groggy the next day.

Furthermore, if you rely on sleep aids like leaving the lights on or having the TV on, you can disrupt your natural sleep cycle. Light exposure, especially blue light from electronic devices, can suppress melatonin production, a hormone that regulates your sleep-wake cycle.

Tips for Regulating Your Sleep Cycle

Here are some tips to help you regulate your sleep cycle and achieve more restful nights:

- **Establish a consistent sleep schedule:** Go to bed and wake up at the same time each day, even on weekends, to regulate your body's natural sleep-wake cycle.

- **Create a relaxing bedtime routine:** Wind down an hour or two before bed with calming activities like reading, taking a warm bath, or listening to relaxing music.

- **Optimize your sleep environment:** Make sure your bedroom is dark, quiet, and cool. Use blackout curtains to block out any light, and consider using earplugs or a white noise machine to minimize noise distractions.

- **Limit screen time before bed:** Avoid using electronic devices for at least an hour before bed. If you must use them, use a blue light filter or wear blue light blocking glasses.

- **Get regular exercise:** Regular physical activity can improve sleep quality, but avoid exercising too close to bedtime.

- **Avoid caffeine and alcohol before bed:** These substances can interfere with your sleep cycle and prevent you from reaching the deeper stages of sleep.

- **Seek professional help if needed:** If you're struggling with chronic sleep problems, consider consulting a sleep specialist or therapist.

By understanding your sleep cycles and implementing these strategies, you can improve your sleep quality, reduce anxiety, and take another step towards overcoming nyctophobia. A well-rested mind and body are better equipped to handle challenges and face fears.

SELF-COMPASSION

You're on quite a journey, facing your fears and learning new ways to cope with the darkness. But in the midst of all this brave work, it's crucial to remember one essential ingredient: self-compassion.

Think about it. How do you usually talk to yourself when you're struggling? Do you berate yourself for feeling afraid? Do you criticize yourself for not making progress fast enough? If so, you're not alone. Many of us have a harsh inner critic that loves to point out our flaws and shortcomings.

But here's the thing: self-criticism doesn't help. In fact, it can actually make things worse. When you're constantly judging yourself, you create a cycle of negativity that can fuel your anxiety and make it harder to overcome your fears.

Self-compassion, on the other hand, is like a warm hug for your soul. It's about treating yourself with the same kindness, understanding, and support that you would offer to a dear friend.

What does self-compassion look like?

It involves three key elements:

1. **Self-kindness:** Instead of judging yourself harshly, offer yourself words of encouragement and understanding. "It's okay to feel afraid. This is a challenging process, but I'm doing my best."

2. **Common humanity:** Recognize that you're not alone in your struggles. Everyone experiences fear and anxiety at some point in their lives. "It's normal to feel this way. Many people struggle with fear of the dark."

3. **Mindfulness:** Observe your thoughts and feelings without judgment. "I'm noticing that I'm feeling anxious right now. That's okay. I can allow this feeling to be present without getting carried away by it."

Why is self-compassion so important?

Research has shown that self-compassion can have a profound impact on our mental and emotional well-being. It can help to:

- Reduce anxiety and depression
- Increase resilience and self-esteem
- Improve motivation and goal achievement
- Strengthen relationships
- Promote feelings of happiness and contentment

How to cultivate self-compassion:

- **Notice your self-talk:** Pay attention to how you talk to yourself throughout the day. Are your thoughts mostly positive and supportive, or are they critical and judgmental?

- **Challenge your inner critic:** When you notice negative self-talk, challenge those thoughts. Ask yourself: "Would I say this to a friend? Is this thought helpful or harmful?"

- **Practice self-kindness:** Treat yourself with the same kindness and understanding that you would offer to a loved one. Offer yourself words of encouragement, forgiveness, and support.

- **Write a self-compassionate letter:** Imagine that you're writing a letter to a friend who is struggling with the same fears as you. What would you say to them? Now, write that same letter to yourself.

- **Use affirmations:** Repeat positive affirmations to yourself daily. "I am strong. I am capable. I am worthy of love and compassion."

- **Engage in activities that nourish your soul:** Make time for activities that bring you joy and help you to connect with yourself. This might include spending time in nature, listening to music, practicing yoga, or pursuing a creative hobby.

Be patient with yourself. Cultivating self-compassion is a process, not a destination. It takes time and practice to shift from self-criticism to self-kindness. But with consistent effort, you can learn to be your own best friend and cheerleader.

Remember, you're not alone on this journey. We all have moments of fear and self-doubt. But by embracing self-compassion, you can create a safe and supportive inner space where you can heal, grow, and truly thrive.

FINDING SUPPORT

We've covered a lot of ground together, haven't we? From understanding the roots of your fear to developing powerful coping strategies, you've been bravely facing the darkness and taking control of your nyctophobia. But you don't have to do it alone.

This chapter is all about the power of connection and the importance of finding support on your journey. Think of it like this: even the bravest mountain climbers rely on a team to reach the summit. They have fellow climbers to encourage them, guides to offer expertise, and a support crew back home cheering them on.

Similarly, as you navigate the challenging terrain of overcoming your fear of the dark, it's essential to build your own support system. Having people to lean on can make all the difference in the world.

Where to find support:

1. Therapy:

A therapist can be an invaluable ally in your journey. They can provide a safe and supportive space to explore your fears, develop personalized coping strategies, and address any underlying anxiety or mental health conditions that may be contributing to your nyctophobia.

Don't hesitate to reach out to a therapist who specializes in anxiety disorders or phobias. They can offer evidence-based treatments like cognitive behavioral therapy (CBT) or exposure therapy, which have been proven effective in helping people overcome their fear of the dark.

2. Support Groups:

Connecting with others who understand what you're going through can be incredibly validating and empowering. Support groups offer a sense of community and shared experience, allowing you to learn from others, share your own struggles, and receive encouragement.

Look for support groups specifically for people with nyctophobia or anxiety disorders. These groups can meet in person or online, providing flexibility and accessibility.

3. Friends and Family:

Don't underestimate the power of your existing support network. Talk to your trusted friends and family members about your fear of the dark. Sharing your vulnerability can strengthen your bonds and create a deeper sense of connection.

Your loved ones can offer emotional support, encouragement, and practical assistance. They can accompany you during exposure exercises, listen without judgment when you need to vent, and celebrate your successes along the way.

4. Online Communities:

In today's digital age, there are countless online communities where you can connect with people who share your experiences. Online forums, social media groups, and dedicated websites can provide a wealth of information, support, and encouragement.

These online communities can be particularly helpful if you don't have access to in-person support groups or if you prefer the anonymity of online interactions.

5. Mentorship:

Consider finding a mentor who has successfully overcome nyctophobia or a similar fear. Their experience and guidance can be invaluable as you navigate your own journey.

A mentor can offer practical advice, share their own story of recovery, and provide inspiration and motivation. They can also help you to stay accountable and committed to your goals.

Reaching out for support is a sign of strength, not weakness. It takes courage to acknowledge your struggles and seek help. By building a strong support system, you'll be creating a safety net that will catch you when you stumble and propel you forward on your path to overcoming nyctophobia.

CREATIVE EXPRESSION

We've explored a lot of practical strategies for overcoming your fear of the dark, from facing your fears head-on to building a supportive community. But sometimes, the most powerful healing comes from tapping into your creative side.

This chapter is all about exploring the therapeutic benefits of creative expression and how it can help you to process your emotions, gain new perspectives, and find freedom from the grip of nyctophobia.

Think of your fear like a tangled knot of emotions, thoughts, and sensations. Creative expression is like gently unraveling that knot, allowing you to understand its complexities and find new ways to release its hold on you.

The Healing Power of Art

Art provides a unique language, a way to communicate what words often cannot express. Whether you're a seasoned artist or someone who hasn't picked up a paintbrush since childhood, there's a creative outlet waiting for you.

Painting, drawing, sculpting, or even creating collages can help you to externalize your fear, giving it a tangible form that you can then explore and transform. You might depict the darkness as a swirling vortex of emotions, a shadowy figure, or an abstract landscape. The act of creating itself can be cathartic, allowing you to release pent-up emotions and gain a sense of control over your fear.

Writing Your Way to Freedom

Writing can be another powerful tool for processing your fear of the dark. Journaling, poetry, or even storytelling can help you to make sense of your experiences, identify patterns, and gain new insights.

You might write about your earliest memories of being afraid of the dark, your most intense fears, or your hopes and dreams for a future free from nyctophobia. As you write, you might be surprised by the emotions and memories that surface. Don't censor yourself; just let the words flow freely.

Other Creative Outlets

Beyond art and writing, there are countless other ways to express your creativity and explore your fear of the dark.

Music can be incredibly therapeutic. Playing an instrument, singing, or even just listening to music can help you to regulate your emotions, reduce anxiety, and find solace. You might create a playlist of songs that evoke feelings of safety and peace, or you might compose your own music to express your journey through nyctophobia.

Dance and movement can also be powerful forms of expression. Moving your body can help you to release tension, connect with your emotions, and find a sense of freedom. You might try dancing in the dark, using your movements to explore your fear and reclaim your space.

Even activities like gardening, cooking, or knitting can be creative outlets. The process of creating something beautiful and tangible can be incredibly satisfying and empowering.

Embrace the Process

The most important thing is to find creative outlets that resonate with you and allow you to express yourself authentically. Don't worry about perfection or judgment. Just allow yourself to explore, experiment, and have fun.

Creative expression is not a magic cure for nyctophobia, but it can be a valuable tool for healing and growth. By tapping into your creativity, you can gain a deeper understanding of your fear, process your emotions, and find new ways to cope. And who knows, you might even discover hidden talents and passions along the way.

STAYING ON TRACK

You've come so far! You've explored the depths of your fear, learned powerful coping strategies, and even started venturing out into the darkness with newfound confidence. But as you continue your journey to overcome nyctophobia, it's important to remember that this is a marathon, not a sprint.

This chapter is all about staying on track, maintaining your momentum, and preventing relapse as you navigate the ups and downs of recovery. Think of it as your guide to long-term success and lasting freedom from the grip of fear.

1. Embrace the Long Haul

Overcoming a phobia like nyctophobia is a process that takes time, patience, and commitment. There will be days when you feel like you're making great strides, and there will be days when you feel like you're taking two steps back. That's perfectly normal.

The key is to remember that progress isn't always linear. Don't get discouraged by setbacks. Instead, view them as opportunities to learn and grow. Each time you face a challenge, you gain valuable experience and resilience.

2. Maintain Your Toolkit

Remember all those amazing tools you've acquired along the way? Keep them handy! Continue to practice the techniques that have helped you so far, such as:

- Challenging your thoughts
- Engaging in relaxation and mindfulness exercises
- Visualizing success
- Utilizing your support system
- Expressing yourself creatively

These tools are your allies in the fight against fear. The more you use them, the stronger they become.

3. Recognize Your Triggers

By now, you're probably quite familiar with the triggers that can set off your fear of the dark. But as you progress, new triggers might emerge, or old ones might resurface. Stay vigilant and be mindful of your reactions.

If you notice yourself feeling anxious in certain situations, take a moment to identify the trigger. Then, use your toolkit to manage your anxiety and prevent it from escalating.

4. Celebrate Your Successes

It's easy to get caught up in the challenges of overcoming nyctophobia, but don't forget to celebrate your successes! Acknowledge your progress, no matter how small it may seem.

Each time you face your fear, whether it's turning off the lights in your bedroom or venturing out for an evening walk, take a moment to appreciate your courage and resilience. Reward yourself for your efforts, and allow yourself to feel proud of how far you've come.

5. Practice Self-Care

Self-care is essential for maintaining your mental and emotional well-being, especially during challenging times. Make sure you're prioritizing activities that nourish your mind, body, and soul.

This might include getting enough sleep, eating a healthy diet, exercising regularly, spending time in nature, connecting with loved ones, or pursuing hobbies and interests that bring you joy.

6. Be Kind to Yourself

Remember that self-compassion is crucial throughout this journey. Don't beat yourself up if you have setbacks or experience moments of fear. Treat yourself with the same kindness and understanding that you would offer to a friend.

Remember, you're not alone in this. Many people struggle with fear of the dark. By practicing self-compassion, you can create a supportive inner environment that fosters healing and growth.

7. Seek Support When Needed

Even with the best intentions and efforts, there might be times when you need extra support. Don't hesitate to reach out to your therapist, support group, or loved ones if you're feeling overwhelmed or struggling to stay on track.

Remember, asking for help is a sign of strength, not weakness. By leaning on your support system, you can navigate challenges and stay committed to your recovery.

Overcoming nyctophobia is a journey that requires ongoing effort and commitment. But by embracing these strategies, you can maintain your progress, prevent relapse, and create a life filled with light, even in the darkest of times.

NIGHTTIME RITUALS

Remember how we talked about creating a sleep sanctuary in your bedroom? Well, this chapter builds on that idea, but instead of focusing on the physical space, we're going to delve into the power of nighttime rituals.

Think of a nighttime ritual as a series of intentional actions you perform before bed to signal to your mind and body that it's time to wind down and prepare for sleep. It's like a gentle lullaby for your soul, easing you into the embrace of the night.

Why are nighttime rituals so important, especially for those of us overcoming nyctophobia?

Firstly, they provide a sense of structure and predictability. When you have a set routine, your mind knows what to expect, reducing anxiety and promoting a feeling of safety and control. This is particularly helpful when dealing with fear of the dark, as it can help to alleviate the uncertainty and apprehension that often accompany nightfall.

Secondly, nighttime rituals help to shift your mindset from the busyness of the day to a state of relaxation and receptivity. By engaging in calming activities, you're essentially telling your nervous system, "It's time to switch gears. It's time to let go of the day's worries and embrace the tranquility of the night."

So, what does a powerful nighttime ritual look like? Well, it's highly personal and can evolve as you do. But here are some ideas to get you started:

1. Disconnect from the Digital World:

At least an hour before bed, start disconnecting from the digital world. Put away your phone, turn off the TV, and close your laptop. The blue light emitted from these devices can interfere with your sleep and keep your mind buzzing.

2. Engage in Calming Activities:

This is where you get to curate your own personal wind-down routine. What activities help you to relax and de-stress? Some popular options include:

- Taking a warm bath with soothing essential oils
- Reading a book (avoid anything too stimulating or suspenseful)
- Listening to calming music or nature sounds
- Practicing gentle yoga or stretching
- Journaling or writing in a gratitude diary
- Spending time in quiet reflection or meditation

3. Dim the Lights:

As you approach bedtime, gradually dim the lights in your home. This mimics the natural dimming of daylight and signals to your body that it's time to produce melatonin, the sleep-regulating hormone.

4. Practice Relaxation Techniques:

Incorporate relaxation techniques into your nighttime ritual to further calm your mind and body. This might include deep breathing exercises, progressive muscle relaxation, or mindfulness meditation.

5. Prepare for the Next Day:

Take a few minutes to prepare for the next day. This might involve laying out your clothes, packing your lunch, or making a to-do list. This can help to clear your mind and reduce any lingering anxieties about the day ahead.

6. Embrace the Darkness:

As you settle into bed, take a moment to appreciate the darkness.

Instead of fearing it, try to view it as a time for rest, rejuvenation, and connection with your inner self. You might even try visualizing your safe and peaceful sanctuary, as we discussed in Chapter 9.

Consistency is Key:

The most important aspect of a nighttime ritual is consistency. Try to perform your routine at the same time each night, even on weekends. This will help to regulate your sleep-wake cycle and create a sense of predictability that can ease your anxiety.

Creating a personalized nighttime ritual is a powerful way to reclaim your relationship with the night. It's a way to honor your need for rest and create a sense of peace and tranquility as you transition from the busyness of the day to the stillness of the night.

EMBRACE THE NIGHT

We've spent a lot of time in this book talking about managing fear, challenging thoughts, and developing coping strategies. But now, let's shift our perspective a bit. Let's talk about not just conquering the darkness, but actually *embracing* the night.

It might sound strange at first, especially if you've spent years dreading the nightfall. But what if, instead of seeing the darkness as an enemy, we could learn to see it as a friend? What if we could find beauty, peace, and even magic in the absence of light?

Think about it. Throughout history, the night has been a source of wonder and inspiration. Poets have written odes to the moon, artists have captured the ethereal beauty of starlight, and musicians have composed symphonies inspired by the sounds of the night.

The night is a time of mystery and enchantment. It's a time when the world slows down, and we can connect with our inner selves on a deeper level. It's a time for reflection, for dreaming, for rejuvenation.

So how can we, as people who have struggled with nyctophobia, learn to embrace the night?

1. Shift Your Perspective:

Start by challenging the negative associations you have with the dark. Instead of seeing it as a source of fear and danger, try to see it as a time of peace and tranquility. Remind yourself that the darkness is a natural part of the cycle of life, just like the daylight.

2. Appreciate the Beauty of the Night:

Take some time to truly appreciate the beauty of the night. Gaze up at the stars, marvel at the moon's glow, and listen to the symphony of nocturnal creatures. You might be surprised by the wonders you discover when you open your senses to the night.

3. Connect with Nature:

Spend time in nature at night. Go for a walk under the moonlight, sit by a campfire, or simply lie in your backyard and gaze up at the stars. Connecting with nature can help you to feel grounded and connected to something larger than yourself.

4. Create a Nighttime Ritual:

As we discussed in the previous chapter, creating a calming nighttime ritual can help you to transition from the busyness of the day to the stillness of the night. This ritual can include activities that help you to connect with the darkness in a positive way, such as stargazing, listening to calming music, or practicing mindfulness meditation.

5. Find Joy in Nighttime Activities:

Explore activities that you can enjoy specifically at night. This might include attending a nighttime yoga class, going for a night swim, visiting a planetarium, or simply enjoying a quiet evening at home with a good book.

6. Embrace the Stillness:

The night offers a unique opportunity to disconnect from the hustle and bustle of daily life and embrace stillness. Use this time for introspection, journaling, or simply enjoying the quietude.

7. Cultivate Gratitude:

As you embrace the night, cultivate a sense of gratitude for the darkness. Appreciate its role in the natural world and its ability to provide rest and rejuvenation.

Embracing the night is a journey that takes time and patience. It's about shifting your perspective, appreciating the beauty of the darkness, and finding ways to connect with the night on a deeper level.

As you learn to embrace the night, you'll not only be overcoming your fear of the dark, but you'll also be opening yourself up to a whole new world of wonder and possibility. You'll be reclaiming the night as a time for peace, rejuvenation, and connection with your inner self.

CELEBRATE SUCCESS

Take a moment to pause and reflect on how far you've come. You've delved into the depths of your fear, learned powerful coping strategies, built a supportive community, and even started embracing the beauty of the night. That's something to celebrate!

This chapter is all about acknowledging your achievements, honoring your resilience, and recognizing the incredible transformation you've undergone on your journey to overcome nyctophobia.

It's easy to get so caught up in the day-to-day challenges of facing your fears that you forget to acknowledge your progress. But celebrating your successes, no matter how small they may seem, is crucial for maintaining motivation and building confidence.

Think back to where you were at the beginning of this journey. Perhaps you were afraid to be alone in the dark, struggled to fall asleep, or avoided social situations that took place at night. Now, look at how far you've come! You're facing your fears, embracing new experiences, and reclaiming your life from the grip of nyctophobia.

Every step you take, every challenge you overcome, is a victory worth celebrating. It's a testament to your courage, your determination, and your unwavering commitment to overcoming your fear.

So how can you celebrate your successes in a meaningful way?

Acknowledge Your Achievements:

Start by simply acknowledging your achievements, both big and small. Each time you face a fear, whether it's turning off the lights in your bedroom or venturing out for an evening walk, take a moment to acknowledge your bravery and resilience. Say to yourself, "I did it! I faced my fear, and I came out stronger."

Keep a Success Journal:

Consider keeping a success journal where you record your accomplishments, no matter how small they may seem. This journal can serve as a tangible reminder of your progress and a source of inspiration when you face challenges along the way.

Share Your Victories with Others:

Share your victories with your support system. Tell your therapist, your friends, your family, or your online community about the progress you're making. Their encouragement and celebration will amplify your own sense of accomplishment.

Reward Yourself:

Treat yourself to something special when you reach a milestone in your journey. This could be a small treat, like a relaxing bath or a delicious meal, or a larger reward, like a weekend getaway or a new hobby.

Practice Gratitude:

Take time to express gratitude for your progress and for the people who have supported you along the way. Gratitude can foster a sense of positivity and appreciation, further enhancing your sense of accomplishment.

Reflect on Your Growth:

Reflect on how far you've come and how much you've grown throughout this journey. Acknowledge the challenges you've overcome, the lessons you've learned, and the strength you've discovered within yourself.

Embrace the Future with Confidence:

As you celebrate your successes, look to the future with confidence and optimism. You've proven to yourself that you can overcome your fear of the dark. Now, embrace the possibilities that lie ahead, knowing that you have the tools and the resilience to face whatever challenges may come your way.

Celebrating your successes is not just about acknowledging your achievements; it's about honoring your journey, recognizing your strength, and embracing the future with hope and excitement. You've earned it!

HELPING OTHERS

You've journeyed through the darkness, faced your fears, and emerged stronger on the other side. You've learned to manage your anxiety, build a supportive community, and even find beauty in the night. Now, it's time to consider how you can use your experience to help others who are still struggling with nyctophobia.

This chapter is all about paying it forward, sharing your story, and offering support and encouragement to those who are navigating the same challenges you once faced.

Think about it. When you were first grappling with your fear of the dark, wouldn't it have been helpful to hear from someone who had successfully overcome it? Wouldn't it have been comforting to know that you weren't alone, that there was hope for a brighter future?

Now, you have the opportunity to be that source of hope and inspiration for others. By sharing your story and offering support, you can make a real difference in the lives of those who are still struggling.

Sharing Your Story:

One of the most powerful ways to help others is by sharing your own story of overcoming nyctophobia. Your experiences, your struggles, and your triumphs can offer hope and encouragement to those who are just beginning their journey.

You can share your story in a variety of ways:

- **Talk to friends and family:** Start by sharing your story with your loved ones. Let them know how you overcame your fear and what strategies helped you the most.

- **Join a support group:** Share your experiences with others in a support group setting. Your insights and encouragement can be invaluable to those who are still struggling.
- **Write a blog or article:** Share your story online through a blog or article. Your words can reach a wider audience and offer hope to people around the world.
- **Give a talk or presentation:** If you're comfortable with public speaking, consider giving a talk or presentation about your experience with nyctophobia. Your story can inspire and motivate others to take action.
- **Mentor someone:** Offer to mentor someone who is struggling with fear of the dark. Your guidance and support can make a significant difference in their journey.

Offering Support and Encouragement:

In addition to sharing your story, you can offer support and encouragement to others in a variety of ways:

- **Listen with empathy:** When someone shares their struggles with you, listen with empathy and understanding. Let them know that you hear them and that you care.
- **Offer practical advice:** Share the strategies and techniques that helped you overcome your fear. Offer practical advice on how to manage anxiety, build a support system, and embrace the night.
- **Provide encouragement:** Remind others that they are not alone and that they can overcome their fear. Offer words of encouragement and support, especially during challenging times.
- **Celebrate their successes:** Celebrate the progress that others make in their journey. Acknowledge their courage and resilience, and remind them of how far they've come.
- **Be a role model:** By living a life free from the limitations of nyctophobia, you can be a powerful role model for others. Show them that it's possible to overcome their fear and live a full and meaningful life.

The Ripple Effect:

When you help others, you not only make a difference in their lives, but you also create a ripple effect that extends far beyond your immediate reach. Your actions can inspire others to pay it forward, creating a chain of support and encouragement that can transform countless lives.

By sharing your story and offering support, you're not just helping others to overcome their fear of the dark; you're also contributing to a world where people feel more connected, supported, and empowered to face their challenges.

So, embrace the opportunity to make a difference. Share your story, offer support, and be a beacon of hope for those who are still navigating the darkness. Your journey has the power to illuminate the path for others and inspire them to find their own way out of the shadows.

NYCTOPHOBIA IN CHILDREN

While fear of the dark is a common experience for many children, for some, it can develop into a full-blown phobia that significantly impacts their lives. This chapter is dedicated to parents, caregivers, and educators who are seeking to understand and support children struggling with nyctophobia.

It's important to remember that children experience fear differently than adults. Their imaginations are vivid, their understanding of the world is still developing, and they often lack the coping mechanisms that adults have acquired over time.

So, how can you tell if a child's fear of the dark is something more than a typical childhood phase?

Here are some signs to watch for:

- **Intense and persistent fear:** The child expresses extreme fear of the dark that persists for an extended period, even after reassurance and comfort.
- **Avoidance behaviors:** The child avoids situations involving darkness, such as bedtime, going to the bathroom alone at night, or participating in nighttime activities.
- **Physical symptoms:** The child experiences physical symptoms of anxiety, such as a racing heart, trembling, sweating, or difficulty breathing, when in the dark.
- **Sleep disturbances:** The child has trouble falling asleep or staying asleep, often waking up with nightmares or night terrors.
- **Impact on daily life:** The child's fear of the dark interferes with their daily activities, school performance, and social

interactions.

If you notice these signs in a child, it's important to take their fear seriously and offer support and guidance. Here are some strategies that can help:

1. Create a Safe and Supportive Environment:

Start by creating a safe and supportive environment where the child feels heard and understood. Validate their fear and let them know that it's okay to feel afraid. Avoid dismissing their fear or making them feel ashamed.

2. Build a Sense of Security:

Help the child to build a sense of security in their bedroom and other areas of the home. This might involve using a nightlight, leaving a door slightly ajar, or providing a comforting object, like a stuffed animal or blanket.

3. Establish a Consistent Routine:

A predictable bedtime routine can help to reduce anxiety and promote a sense of safety. This might include a warm bath, reading a story, or singing a lullaby.

4. Gradual Exposure:

Gradually expose the child to the darkness in a safe and controlled manner. Start with small steps, such as dimming the lights for a few minutes each night, and gradually increase the duration as the child becomes more comfortable.

5. Use Play and Storytelling:

Engage the child in play and storytelling to help them process their fear and develop coping strategies. Use puppets, dolls, or drawings to create stories about overcoming fear and facing challenges.

6. Empower the Child:

Empower the child by giving them choices and control over their environment. Let them choose their nightlight, their bedtime story, or their comforting object. This can help to build their confidence and sense of agency.

7. Seek Professional Help:

If the child's fear is severe or persistent, consider seeking professional help from a therapist who specializes in child anxiety disorders. A therapist can provide evidence-based treatments, such as cognitive behavioral therapy (CBT) or play therapy, to help the child overcome their fear.

8. Be Patient and Understanding:

Remember that overcoming a fear takes time and patience. Be patient and understanding with the child, and celebrate their successes along the way. Offer encouragement and support, and remind them that they are loved and capable of overcoming their fear.

By creating a supportive environment, implementing effective strategies, and seeking professional help when needed, you can help a child overcome their fear of the dark and develop a healthy relationship with the night.

THE SCIENCE OF FEAR

We've explored the emotional and practical aspects of nyctophobia, but have you ever wondered what's happening in your brain when you feel that surge of fear in the dark? This chapter takes a peek behind the curtain to explore the fascinating science of fear, specifically how it relates to your fear of the dark.

Understanding the biological mechanisms at play can demystify your experience and empower you to take control. Think of it like this: knowing how a car engine works doesn't necessarily make you a mechanic, but it can help you understand why your car sputters when it's low on fuel. Similarly, understanding the science of fear can provide valuable insights into why your body reacts the way it does in the dark.

The Amygdala: Your Brain's Alarm System

Deep within your brain, nestled in a structure called the limbic system, lies the amygdala. This almond-shaped cluster of neurons acts as your brain's alarm system, constantly scanning for potential threats. When it perceives danger, it triggers a cascade of physiological responses that prepare you to fight, flee, or freeze.

Think of the amygdala as a vigilant guard dog. It's always on alert, ready to bark at the first sign of trouble. In the context of nyctophobia, the darkness itself can become the trigger that sets off the alarm.

The Fight-or-Flight Response

When the amygdala perceives a threat, it sends signals to the hypothalamus, a control center in your brain that regulates various bodily functions. The hypothalamus, in turn, activates the sympathetic nervous system, triggering the release of stress hormones like adrenaline and cortisol.

These hormones prepare your body for action. Your heart rate increases, your breathing becomes rapid, your muscles tense, and your senses sharpen. This is the fight-or-flight response, an evolutionary mechanism designed to help you survive in dangerous situations.

However, in the case of nyctophobia, this response is often triggered inappropriately. Your brain misinterprets the darkness as a threat, even though there's no real danger present. This can lead to a cycle of anxiety and fear, as your body's physical reactions reinforce your perception of the darkness as something to be feared.

The Role of the Hippocampus

Another important player in the fear response is the hippocampus, a seahorse-shaped structure involved in learning and memory. The hippocampus helps to contextualize your fears, associating them with specific places, situations, or events.

For example, if you had a frightening experience in the dark as a child, your hippocampus might have created a strong association between darkness and fear. This association can trigger an anxiety response even when you're in a safe environment.

Neuroplasticity: Rewiring Your Brain

The good news is that your brain is incredibly adaptable. Through a process called neuroplasticity, your brain can rewire itself, forming new neural pathways and weakening old ones. This means that you can learn to overcome your fear of the dark by repeatedly exposing yourself to it in a safe and controlled manner.

As you engage in exposure therapy and other coping strategies, your brain begins to recognize that the darkness is not a threat. The amygdala becomes less reactive, the fight-or-flight response diminishes, and the hippocampus forms new associations between darkness and safety.

Understanding the science of fear can be empowering. It helps you to see your fear not as a personal failing, but as a natural biological response that can be modified through learning and experience. By understanding the intricate workings of your brain, you can take control of your fear and create a brighter future, free from the shadows of nyctophobia.

RESOURCES AND FURTHER READING

You've come a long way on your journey to overcome nyctophobia. You've explored the nature of your fear, learned practical strategies for managing anxiety, and even discovered ways to embrace the darkness. But the journey doesn't have to end here.

This chapter is your guide to further exploration, providing a wealth of resources to support your continued growth and deepen your understanding of nyctophobia. Think of it as a treasure map, leading you to valuable information, support networks, and inspiring stories.

Books:

- **"Overcoming Fear of the Dark" by Dr. David Veale and Rob Willson:** This book offers a comprehensive cognitive behavioral therapy (CBT) approach to overcoming nyctophobia, with practical exercises and techniques to manage anxiety and face your fears.
- **"Darkness Visible: A Memoir of Madness" by William Styron:** While not specifically about nyctophobia, this powerful memoir offers a profound exploration of depression and the darkness that can envelop the human spirit.
- **"The Power of Now" by Eckhart Tolle:** This spiritual guide emphasizes the importance of mindfulness and present moment awareness, which can be invaluable in managing anxiety and fear.

Websites and Organizations:

- **Anxiety and Depression Association of America (ADAA):** This website provides a wealth of information about anxiety disorders, including nyctophobia, along with resources for finding therapists and support groups.
- **The National Institute of Mental Health (NIMH):** This website offers reliable information about mental health conditions, including anxiety disorders, and research-based treatments.
- **The Darkness Foundation:** This organization is dedicated to raising awareness about nyctophobia and providing support and resources to those affected by it.

Apps:

- **Calm:** This popular app offers guided meditations, sleep stories, and relaxation music to help you manage anxiety and improve sleep quality.
- **Headspace:** This app provides mindfulness exercises and meditation techniques to cultivate present moment awareness and reduce stress.
- **Insight Timer:** This app offers a vast library of guided meditations, talks, and music from various teachers and traditions.

Connect with Others:

Remember the power of community and shared experience. Reach out to others who have overcome nyctophobia or are currently navigating their journey. Share your story, offer support, and learn from their experiences. Online forums, social media groups, and support groups can provide a sense of connection and belonging.

Continue Learning:

The more you learn about nyctophobia, the better equipped you'll be to manage your fear and support your continued growth.

Read books, articles, and research studies. Attend workshops and conferences. Stay curious and keep exploring.

This journey of overcoming nyctophobia is an ongoing process of self-discovery, learning, and growth. Embrace the resources available to you, continue to deepen your understanding, and celebrate your progress along the way. You have the power to create a life filled with light, even in the darkest of times.

FREQUENTLY ASKED QUESTIONS ABOUT NYCTOPHOBIA

As you've journeyed through this book, you've likely had questions pop up along the way. This chapter is dedicated to answering some of the most frequently asked questions about nyctophobia, offering clarity and reassurance as you continue your journey to overcome your fear of the dark.

1. Is nyctophobia common?

Yes, nyctophobia is more common than you might think. While it's often associated with childhood, it can affect people of all ages. Many adults struggle with fear of the dark, and it's important to remember that you're not alone in this experience.

2. What's the difference between a normal fear of the dark and nyctophobia?

It's perfectly natural to experience some apprehension or discomfort in the dark, especially as a child. However, nyctophobia is characterized by an intense, irrational fear that significantly impacts your daily life. If your fear of the dark prevents you from engaging in activities, disrupts your sleep, or causes significant distress, it's important to seek support and consider professional help.

3. Can nyctophobia be cured?

While there's no magic cure for nyctophobia, it is a treatable condition. With the right tools and strategies, you can learn to manage your anxiety, face your fears, and ultimately overcome your fear of the dark. This book has provided you with a comprehensive toolkit to support you on this journey.

4. How long does it take to overcome nyctophobia?

The journey to overcome nyctophobia is unique for each individual. Some people may experience significant improvement within a few weeks or months, while others may require a longer period of dedicated effort. The key is to be patient with yourself, celebrate your progress, and seek support when needed.

5. What if I have setbacks?

Setbacks are a normal part of the recovery process. Don't be discouraged if you experience moments of fear or anxiety. Instead, view these setbacks as opportunities to learn and grow. Use your coping strategies, lean on your support system, and remember how far you've already come.

6. Will I always be afraid of the dark?

While it's possible that you may always experience some degree of apprehension in the dark, you can learn to manage your fear and prevent it from controlling your life. With consistent effort and the right support, you can create a life where the darkness no longer holds you back.

7. What if my child is afraid of the dark?

If your child is struggling with fear of the dark, it's important to offer support, validation, and reassurance. Create a safe and comforting environment, establish a consistent bedtime routine, and consider seeking professional help if the fear is severe or persistent.

8. Is medication helpful for nyctophobia?

In some cases, medication may be helpful in managing anxiety and promoting sleep. However, medication should always be used in conjunction with therapy and other coping strategies.

Consult with a qualified healthcare professional to determine if medication is right for you.

9. What if I can't afford therapy?

If you're unable to afford traditional therapy, there are still many resources available to you. Consider seeking support from community mental health centers, online support groups, or self-help resources.

10. What's the most important thing to remember when overcoming nyctophobia?

The most important thing to remember is that you are not alone. Many people struggle with fear of the dark, and there is help available. Be kind to yourself, celebrate your progress, and believe in your ability to overcome this challenge.

This chapter has provided answers to some of the most common questions about nyctophobia. If you have further questions or concerns, don't hesitate to reach out to a qualified healthcare professional or mental health provider.

A FINAL WORD:
EMBRACE THE NIGHT
AND LIVE YOUR LIFE
TO THE FULLEST

As we reach the end of this journey together, it's time for a final reflection, a moment to acknowledge the incredible transformation you've undergone. You began this book perhaps hesitant, unsure, maybe even a little afraid of the very darkness we've explored. But look at you now!

You've delved into the depths of your fear, understanding its origins and its impact on your life. You've learned to challenge your thoughts, manage your anxiety, and face the darkness with newfound courage. You've built a supportive community, embraced creative expression, and even discovered the beauty and tranquility that the night has to offer.

You've learned that the darkness is not something to be feared, but rather a natural part of life's rhythm, a time for rest, reflection, and rejuvenation. You've learned that you are stronger than your fear, that you have the power to overcome challenges and create a life filled with light, even in the darkest of times.

But most importantly, you've learned that you are not alone. Many people share this journey with you, facing their own fears and seeking a brighter future. And as you continue to move forward, remember that the tools and strategies you've acquired in this book are yours to keep.

Continue to practice self-compassion, nurture your support system, and embrace the creative outlets that bring you joy. Stay mindful of your thoughts and feelings, and don't hesitate to seek support when needed.

As you step out into the world, remember that the darkness no longer holds you captive. You have the power to choose how you respond to it. You can choose to see it as a source of fear, or you can choose to see it as an opportunity for growth, reflection, and connection with your inner self.

Embrace the night. Embrace the stillness. Embrace the unknown. For it is in the darkness that we often find our greatest strength, our deepest wisdom, and our most profound connections.

This is not the end of your journey, but rather a new beginning. A beginning filled with hope, possibility, and the freedom to live your life to the fullest, no longer limited by the shadows of fear.

Go forth and shine your light, knowing that you have the power to illuminate not only your own path but also the paths of others who are still navigating the darkness.